I0426366

JPAC Fiscal 2010 Annual Report

Presented by
MG Stephen Tom

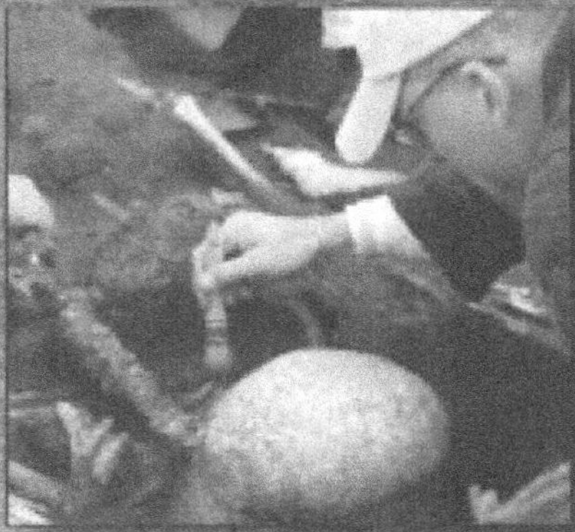

Executive Summary

As the Department of Defense's primary mechanism to account for American's lost in past wars, the Joint POW/MIA Accounting Command continued to make strong advances toward fulfilling its mission during Fiscal 2010.

Since 1 October 2009, we have identified 67 individuals including one from World War I, 36 from World War II, 17 from the Korean War, and 13 from the Vietnam War. We deployed 77 JPAC teams to such places as France, Germany, Belgium, Austria, Papua New Guinea, Vanuatu, China, South Korea, Vietnam, Laos, and Cambodia to conduct investigation, survey, and excavation operations associated to missing Americans. Despite being informed early this year that the use of foreign non-Commercial Airlift Review Board (CARB) approved carriers for personnel transportation is not permitted, we successfully adapted our plan to ensure no loss of operations tempo occurred. Additionally, JPAC complied with a FY 2010 National Defense Authorization Act (NDAA) Sense of Congress to pursue U.S. Marines lost during World War II on Tarawa, Republic of Kiribati. JPAC excavated and closed five sites on this island and plans to conduct research and return to continue field work in the future.

Our Central Identification Laboratory (CIL) advanced new and promising identification techniques involving radiographic comparison and facial superimposition. In fact, the radiographic comparison technique was applied for the first time ever to the identification of a Korean War loss whose remains were not viable for mtDNA testing. In the coming years, we anticipate that this technique will drastically increase our ability to identify servicemen for whom mtDNA matching is not an alternative. Our scientists also furthered research in the areas of skeletal trauma and stature estimation that will not only aid in the identification of fallen servicemen, but will contribute to the body of scientific techniques available to the larger forensic community. We are proud to have expanded scientific interaction and collaboration through our Forensic Science Academy (FSA), now in its third year, in the form of more in depth interactions between JPAC fellows and scientists with the staff at the Khon Kaen University in Thailand.

Our Intelligence Directorate raced ahead in their application of Geographic Information Systems (GIS) by developing meaningful products to support interagency and diplomatic interactions, case analysis, survey recording, recovery mission preparation, and operational planning among other areas. Additionally, despite a demanding investigative deployment schedule and ongoing research/case development imperatives, our Southeast Asia, Korean War and World War II analysts and historians presented a total of 50 cases for excavation consideration.

Our External Relations program saw increased interaction with Congress, family members and the public. In fact, almost 600 requests for information (compared to 387 last year) were processed reflecting a sharp increase in external interest and engagement. In concert with other members of the accounting community such as the Defense Prisoner of War/Missing Personnel Office (DPMO), the Armed Forces DNA Identification Laboratory (AFDIL), and representatives from each branch of service, JPAC participated in nine family update meetings across the U.S. to engage with family members one-on-one. Interaction with Congress was also prominent as in years past. JPAC hosted two House Armed Services Committee staff members on a tour of excavation sites in Korea and Vietnam then arranged their visit with a variety of staff members at our headquarters, offering a firsthand look at our operation. To complement these efforts, JPAC hosted over 100 public tours at our headquarters and participated in a variety of Veterans or similar events throughout the country. We also launched a social media initiative this year; in just a few months we gained over 300 followers on Facebook and have seen significant activity on our Twitter site. It seems inevitable that public and family exchanges will increase in the coming years due to our participation in social networking. We hope to reach new family members and promote knowledge and unprecedented exposure of our mission through this communication platform.

In addition to the aforementioned novel undertakings, we devoted time and energy to improving outcomes for existing programs. We bolstered our underwater excavation capability by recruiting two new underwater archaeologists, streamlined the records request process, and have improved our physical and intellectual control over our records. Our Policy and Negotiations Directorate also led our participation in the "Equip and Train" program in which JPAC donated Global Positioning System (GPS) and other equipment to our counterparts in Papua New Guinea (PNG). This should not only ensure better data collection and documentation, but will reinforce our relationships with our foreign partners which will ultimately advance our success in that country. We will continue to seek and capitalize on opportunities with not only a direct but also an indirect benefit to our mission. The importance of strengthening partnerships to maximize our effectiveness simply cannot be understated in the context of a rapidly developing world and potentially disappearing loss sites.

I received excellent support toward our personnel accounting efforts from the U.S. Pacific Command, Joint Staff, Ambassadors, Defense Attaché's, and the Armed Forces throughout my first year as JPAC commander. These entities have proven to be a crucial component to JPAC's operational success and I appreciate the support from these partners. I am also honored that Secretary of State Hillary Rodham-Clinton attended the Repatriation Ceremony in Vietnam; it demonstrates the strong level of interest and support we receive from the very highest levels of our National government.

The recent passage of the FY2010 National Defense Authorization Act created a new paradigm for the accounting community. I am open to creative and thoughtful approaches to reach 200 annual identifications by 2015. I recognize that compliance with this legislation compels collaboration with our partners and stakeholders and I welcome the dialogue.

I am deeply honored to have been given command over such a noble mission and highly skilled staff. I look forward with tremendous optimism to another year of accomplishments in FY 2011.

Until They Are Home!

STEPHEN D. TOM
Major General, U.S. Army
Commander, Joint POW/MIA
Accounting Command

TABLE OF CONTENTS

MISSION

JPAC conducts global operations in support of achieving the fullest possible accounting of personnel unaccounted-for as a result of the nation's past conflicts. JPAC's functions include case analysis; archival research; host nation operational/technical talks; field investigations; excavations; recoveries; remains repatriation, personal identifications and reporting.

TARAWA, Republic of Kiribati (Sept. 20, 2010) - A Marine detail from 2nd Marine Division and Marine Forces Pacific conducts a repatriation ceremony on the island of Tarawa, Republic of Kiribati. (JPAC photo by Marine Corps Staff Sgt. Adaecus G. Brooks).

IDENTIFICATIONS

In FY10, JPAC identified 17 individuals from the Vietnam War, 18 from the Korean War and 36 from World War II. While, the Central Identification Laboratory identifies about two Americans a week, the recovery and identification process may take years to complete. Once a case is completed, the military service branch's Casualty Office notifies families personally of the identification. It is not until a family member accepts an identification that the Department of Defense publically announces the identification and updates the unaccounted for statistics.

Congress, through the FY2010 National Defense Authorization Act, has asked the Secretary of Defense to "increase significantly the capability and capacity of the Department of Defense, the Armed Forces, and commanders of the combatant commands to account for missing persons so that, beginning with fiscal year 2015, the POW/MIA accounting community has sufficient resources to ensure that at least 200 individuals are accounted for under the program annually." JPAC and our counterparts across the accounting community have begun evaluating the options for complying with this legislation. While there is still much planning and analysis to be done, it seems clear that action is required immediately in order to generate the required inputs to accomplish such an increase in output and productivity. We will continue to study this issue and

Anthropologist Owen O'Leary, far left, and U.S. Navy Chief Petty Officer William Eickhoff, right, train the recovery team and the Indian soldiers for a medical evacuation in Arunachal Pradesh, India, on November, 2009. (JPAC Photo by U.S. Marine Corps Sgt. Neill A. Sevelius).

collaborate with our partners in the accounting community to determine the most appropriate course of action.

OPERATIONS

WORLD WAR II

Approximately 74,000 individuals remain unaccounted for from World War II. Thus far, 544 individuals have been identified and repatriated and there are currently 61 sites associated with WWII losses waiting to be scheduled for excavation. During fiscal year 2010, JPAC deployed seven Investigation Teams (IT) and 11 Recovery Teams (RT) to areas around the world to work on World War II cases.

Our WWII Intelligence Analysts and historians have sustained a significant and diverse workload this fiscal year. While supporting ongoing planning efforts and managing the rapidly increasing amount of new information coming in for WWII, they successfully transitioned 14 cases onto the excavation list enabling the progression of two cases in Papua New Guinea, seven in Germany, one in China, one in Bulgaria, one in Belgium, and two in Austria into the

next major phase of JPAC work. Four more sites are currently being considered for excavation including two in France, one in Ukraine and one in Bulgaria. If the JPAC Commander determines that enough evidence exists to warrant an excavation, these four cases will be added to the excavation queue and our operations planners will work to schedule recovery operations.

Despite a demanding investigative deployment schedule, our Investigators have also focused on research advances. This fiscal year, they accomplished one archival research trip to Vienna, Austria, one to the National Archives and Records Administration (NARA), two archival research-records collection trips to the National Personnel Records Center (NPRC) in St. Louis, Missouri, one archival research trip to the SeaBees Museum in California and one archival research/survey of the records stored at the modern History Branch of the Papua New Guinea National Museum. Through our historian/analysts staff, JPAC continues to interface with a range of third party enthusiasts who provide a large volume of reports and data to JPAC throughout the year. We also continue to

Anthropologist Owen O'Leary, Joint POW/MIA Accounting Command, carves an "X" in a boulder, permanently marking a reference point for future recovery missions in Arunachal Pradesh, India, on November 15, 2009. JPAC Photo by U.S. Marine Corps Sgt. Neill A. Sevelius.

TARAWA, Republic of Kiribati (Sept. 20, 2010) - A recovery team from the Joint POW/MIA Accounting Command renders salutes as a Marine detail from 2nd Marine Division and Marine Forces Pacific passes by with a transfer case during a repatriation ceremony on the island of Tarawa, Republic of Kiribati. (JPAC photo by Marine Corps Staff Sgt. Adaecus G. Brooks).

collaborate with other private researchers including a Pearl Harbor survivor and historian of the Pearl Harbor Survivors Association, who has worked tirelessly to help identify remains from 7 December 1941 that were buried as unknowns at the National Memorial Cemetery of the Pacific.

From October – November 2009, JPAC conducted an excavation at a WWI site in France associated to a ground loss. The individual associated with this site has already been identified and buried at Arlington National Cemetery. A JPAC RT also excavated one site in India for eight unaccounted for but had to suspend work for a future mission. Four European investigations during this timeframe covered a total of 32 cases across Germany, Luxembourg, Belgium, Netherlands, Italy, Austria, Bulgaria, Ukraine, and France throughout the year. From January to February 2010, JPAC recovery teams excavated a site in Madang Province associated with an April 1944 crash of a B-24D Liberator compromised by anti-aircraft fire while on a bombing mission over Hansa Bay, PNG. Work was continued on this site during our August–September mission and all recovered evidence is undergoing analysis in our laboratory. We also recovered evidence at a site in Morobe Province associated to a P-38 crash site. The individual associated to this incident was identified in September 2010. Our investigators worked on eight cases in PNG during this time period to develop additional details that might move cases closer to excavation approval.

In the March–April timeframe, a recovery mission was conducted at the site of a SB2C-5 aircraft which crashed in March 1948 with one crew member aboard in a wooded area south of Wheeler, Oregon. The crew member was previously recovered and identified on 2 April 1948 but the JPAC team recovered what are believed to be additional remains and have closed the site to future excavations. JPAC investigators also investigated four cases in Italy during March–April 2010.

Air Force Senior Master Sgt. Rob Louchery, a medical technician with the Joint POW/MIA Accounting Command, assists in scooping rocks and debris into buckets to prepare the covered surface for excavation outside the province of Gangwon, S. Korea on May 27, 2010. (JPAC photo U.S. Marine Corps Staff Sgt. Adaecus G. Brooks).

In the June–July 2010 timeframe, a survey team conducted work in Malaysia at a site associated with a C47-B aircraft involving three unaccounted for service members. We also excavated and recovered possible remains from two sites in Vanuatu; one was from the crash site of a TBF-1 with two unaccounted for crewmen and the other from a case which involved a PB1-J with seven unaccounted for crew members. Work at both sites will be resumed on a future mission. Also during this period in Germany, teams excavated an isolated burial at Nideggenerstrasse, Germany (no evidence recovered). We also excavated and recovered possible remains at a site believed to be associated to a November 1944 ground loss involving a

26th Infantry Regiment attack in Merode Village, Germany for which one soldier is still unaccounted-for. Additionally, teams excavated a site believed to be associated to a December 1944 air loss of nine crewmembers onboard a B-26C aircraft that crashed due to enemy fire while on a bombing mission to Mayern, Germany. The crash resulted in six survivors. A subsequent recovery operation resulted in the resolution of one individual but two men are still unaccounted-for from that incident. Evidence from these sites is currently undergoing analysis in our laboratory. Our investigation teams investigated nine cases in Germany during July 2010.

From August–September, JPAC excavated the site of a B-24 with nine unaccounted for in Morobe Province, PNG but recovered no evidence. Teams also continued work on the site that we started excavating in January–February involving the crash of a B-24D Liberator. Nine Americans associated with this incident are currently unaccounted-for. Also during this timeframe, JPAC sent a recovery team to Tarawa, Republic of Kiribati in search of the remains associated with the November 1943 loss of Marines from the 2nd Marine Division performing combat operations against Japanese. Approximately 510 U.S. Marines are still unaccounted-for from that engagement. Evidence from this mission is currently

Army Capt. Marymaureene Lirio, team leader of a 12-personnel recovery team of the Joint POW/MIA Accounting Command, shovels excavated soil into buckets for dry screening during a recovery mission outside the province of Gangwon, S. Korea on May 28, 2010. The team deployed out of Joint Base Pearl Harbor-Hickam, Hawaii, to S. Korea for 45 days attempting to recover remains of U.S. service members lost during the Korean War, supporting JPAC's worldwide mission to achieve the fullest possible accounting of those service members lost during our country's previous conflicts. (JPAC photo U.S. Marine Corps Staff Sgt. Adoecus G. Brooks).

undergoing analysis in our laboratory. Investigators worked on 11 cases in Bulgaria, Austria, Germany, and France from August–September 2009. An Investigation Team also deployed to PNG during this period and investigated 11 cases.

THE KOREAN WAR

From the Democratic People's Republic of Korea (DPRK), we identified 121 individuals since 1996 and estimate that 4,573 individuals have yet to be recovered from north of the Korean Demilitarized Zone (DMZ). When directed by higher headquarters, we are prepared to resume operations in the DPRK and will request access to the Unsan area where we were conducting operations before asked to halt field activities in that country.

Currently, 149 individuals of the estimated 8,000 missing have been identified from the Korean War. In FY10, JPAC's Northeast Asia Research and Analysis Section (NEARAS) investigated American losses from the Korean War consisting of five investigation missions in the Republic of Korea (ROK) and two in the People's Republic of China (PRC). JPAC also accomplished six recovery operations and two Joint Forensic Reviews[1] (JFRs) this fiscal year.

Our South Korea investigations approach involved canvassing operations in two large geographic areas; north along the ROK buffer zone (adjacent to the DMZ) and in the south around the area of the Pusan Perimeter. Within these two search areas, our investigators focused on 66 Field Search Cases (FSC) associated with 182 U.S. personnel lost during the Korean War. Altogether, our South Korea FY10 canvassing activities have resulted in more than 5,000 contacts and the development of 30 leads.

Both investigation missions to the PRC involved the survey of a possible crash site for a U.S. aircraft that crashed in November 1950 in Guangdong Province. The success of this investigation resulted in the site being placed on the excavation list. JPAC is currently negotiating/coordinating with the PRC for a recovery mission to occur sometime in FY 2011.

As a result of the above and previous canvassing activities, nine cases were nominated for excavation; eight were approved and placed on the JPAC excavation list and one site believed to be associated to a ROK loss incident was referred to the ROK Ministry of National Defense Agency for Killed in Action Recovery and Identification (MAKRI) for recovery. Additionally, JPAC's NEARAS conducted research and analysis with the Defense POW/Missing Persons Office's (DPMO) Northeast Asia Research and Analysis Section to advance Korean War cases.

---

[1] Joint Forensic Reviews (JFRs) are conducted with host-nation representatives to determine if remains recovered or received are human, to ascertain their evidentiary value (e.g., possible cultural affiliation) in terms of identifying missing Americans and to select and document the condition and approximate number of remains for repatriation to the U.S. for further analysis. They are usually held at a host nation facility and attended by a team of host nation specialists in anthropology, medicine, and/or anatomy, a JPAC anthropologist and possibly a JPAC odontologist, and other members of the JPAC staff.

From March–April 2010, a JPAC excavation team excavated a witness-reported isolated burial in Kyongsang Province reported to us through MAKRI. The team found possible human remains and closed the site to further excavation work. The remains were evaluated during the JFR in August 2010 some were brought back to JPAC for further analysis. The recovery team also excavated an F-80 crash site in Kangwon Province. Although the team found life support and aircraft wreckage, no other evidence was found and the recovery leader closed the site to future excavations.

In April–May, JPAC conducted a survey of a witness-reported site in Kyongsang Province and closed the site having not recovered any evidence.

From May–June 2010, teams excavated and, not having recovered any evidence, closed two isolated burial sites in Kangwon Province. Additionally, a recovery team commenced excavation of a site in North Kyeongsang Province but suspended work because of time constraints and recommended follow on work during a future mission. JPAC also started excavation on what is believed to be a mass grave in Kyongsang Province and plans to continue work there after the landowner has harvested his crops.

Although JPAC has not conducted operations in the DPRK since 2005, we are prepared to resume work at Unsan, Changjin (Chosin) Reservoir, Kujang, and Kunu-ri when directed by higher headquarters. In the meantime, JPAC continues to work with our counterparts at the DPMO in Washington D.C. to refine loss information from these and other battlefields in the DPRK.

THE VIETNAM WAR

Since the signing of the Paris Peace Accords on 27 January 1973, the U.S. government has identified 949 individuals and 1,669 individuals are still unaccounted for from the Southeast Asia (SEA) Conflict. In FY10, JPAC conducted 50 missions in Southeast Asia.

In the Socialist Republic of Vietnam (SRV), the U.S. government has identified 668 Americans and 1,303 Americans are still unaccounted for. In FY10, JPAC identified seven individuals who had been lost in Vietnam. JPAC conducted four SRV Joint Field Activities (JFAs), 13 recovery teams excavated 17 cases and investigated one case, and two investigation teams investigated 101 cases. In January, a small recovery team assisted the Vietnamese Office for Seeking Missing Persons (VNOSMP) recovery team in excavating one crash site. Detachment 2 supported one Trilateral Investigation in Laos and two Trilateral Operations in the Kingdom of Cambodia (KOC). In September, JPAC deployed an additional two-person team that investigated eight cases and on very short notice, two recovery teams excavated one underwater case just off the coast of Thua Thien-Hue Province. Also, during two Investigative Advance Work periods, the Vietnamese investigated 26 cases on our behalf and by doing so contributed to our efforts to maximize productivity on U.S. cases.

During the four JFAs in Vietnam, the VNOSMP conducted a total of 36 unilateral advance work investigations for 24 cases. They also surveyed three restricted sites and excavated two restricted burial areas. They also excavated and recovered human remains at a crash site with the assistance of the small U.S. recovery team mentioned earlier. During FY10, JPAC also conducted Field Forensic Reviews (FFR) both during and outside our JFA. During the FFR's, JPAC jointly examined 18 possible cases with our Vietnamese counterparts to determine which remains would be repatriated to the U.S. The evaluation resulted in 11 cases returning to the JPAC-CIL for further analysis. JPAC conducted one semi-annual technical meeting with the VNOSMP Committee in Hanoi in April and then hosted the meeting in Hawaii in late September. JPAC was also honored to welcome Secretary of State, Mrs. Hillary Rodham-Clinton to attend our final repatriation ceremony of the fiscal year in September.

In the Lao People's Democratic Republic (LPDR), the U.S. government has identified 249 Americans and 330 Americans are still unaccounted for. In FY10, JPAC identified six Americans who were unaccounted for from the LPDR. We conducted five LPDR JFAs; composed of 16 recovery teams that excavated 18 cases and two investigation teams that investigated 19 cases and excavated one case. Our Lao counterparts investigated six cases during their December 2010 IAW timeframe. In February and August, JPAC and Lao Officials held two technical meetings in Vientiane. Also, two separate Civil Aviation Review Board Meetings convened in Vientiane to discuss helicopter support issues.

In the Kingdom of Cambodia (KOC), the U.S. government has identified 32 individuals and 59 Americans are still unaccounted for. JPAC didn't identify anyone unaccounted for from the KOC in FY10. JPAC conducted two KOC JFAs; one recovery team excavated one case and an investigation team investigated three cases. In April, JPAC deployed a recovery team on short notice to excavate the site of a burial that was being destroyed by third country nationals. In July, JPAC conducted its annual technical meeting with the KOC POW/MIA Committee in Siem Reap. In the late summer, a U.S. Navy ship attempted to locate an underwater crash site off-the-coast of Tang Island, but the rough weather conditions prevented them from locating the crash site. In September, a small U.S. /KOC POW/MIA Committee team conducted a trilateral investigation with a Vietnamese witness for one case.

Currently there are seven Americans unaccounted for in the People's Republic of China (PRC). Although JPAC conducted two investigations in the PRC, they have not yet allowed JPAC to conduct investigations associated to the Vietnam War.

UNDERWATER OPERATIONS

JPAC CIL has significantly expanded its underwater capability in 2010. We have completed multiple underwater investigation and recovery missions to include Phase I remote-sensing river and ocean surveys in Cambodia with U.S. Army 7th Engineers; an underwater excavation in Vietnam with Mobile Diving Salvage Unit 1 (MDSU-1) in Hawaii; a Phase II testing and evaluation off the USNS SAFEGUARD near Koh Tang, Cambodia with MDSU-1/Hawaii; and a land and underwater recovery in Vietnam with a MDSU-1/San Diego.

We have also recruited two new underwater archaeologists with specializations in Geographic Information Systems (GIS) and underwater remote-sensing, respectively. Dr. Stefan Claesson comes to us from the Ocean Processes Analysis Laboratory at the University of New Hampshire, and Mr. Andrew Pietrusky will be joining CIL as an Oak Ridge Institute for Science and Education (ORISE) fellow upon completion of his PhD in January 2011. Both of these individuals bring years of underwater survey, investigation, excavation work experience, and expertise to JPAC. In addition, we developed a Dive Operations Specialist position that currently sits at Detachment 4 (JPAC Teams Detachment). Mr. Brick Bradford is a former U.S. Navy Master Diver who brings a wealth of knowledge and experience to the underwater missions planning process.

TARAWA OPERATIONS

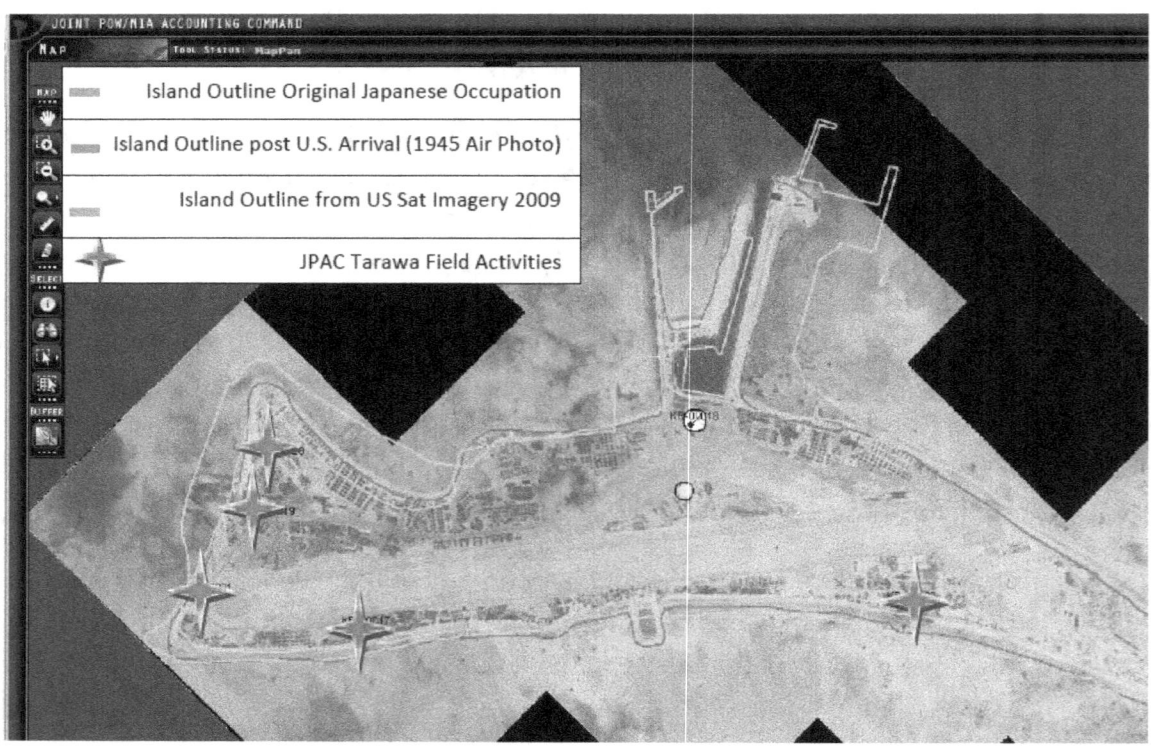

In August–September 2010, a JPAC recovery team excavated 5 of 6 sites approved for excavation on Tarawa in response to a Sense of Congress in the FY10 National Defense Authorization Act to pursue American Marines that may still be buried on this island. The map above depicts JPAC fieldwork locations along with estimated geographic and terrain changes over the years due to construction and development.

From 20–23 November 1943, approximately 1,113 U.S. Marines and sailors were killed during the invasion of Tarawa, Republic of Kiribati (formerly the Gilbert Islands). Island beautification and American Graves Registration (AGRS) activities subsequent to the battle have resulted in the loss of specific cemetery locations. JPAC estimates that between 495 – 510 individuals are unaccounted for from that incident including those who were buried and those that were lost in the water. In addition to the U.S. servicemen believed to be buried on Tarawa, approximately 4,000 Japanese soldiers and 1,000 Korean laborers are also believed to be buried on the 1.5 square mile island.

The National Defense Authorization Act for Fiscal Year 2010 included a Sense of Congress on the recovery of the remains of members of the Armed Forces who were killed during World War II in the battle of Tarawa Atoll. Through this act, Congress encouraged the Department of Defense to "review this research and, as appropriate, pursue new efforts to conduct field studies, new research, and undertake all feasible efforts to recover, identify, and return remains of members of the Armed Forces from Tarawa."

A brief initial survey was conducted in the fall of 2009 on Tarawa to collect a series of reference points that could be used to georeference maps, imagery, and the geophysical survey work conducted previously by a private third party group. This data was used as a baseline to overlay invasion maps, 1945 reconnaissance imagery, as well as modern imagery and public works data.

In August–September 2010, a JPAC RT excavated six sites on the island in search of the remains of U.S. service members from the 1943 invasion. While the team located a mass burial of Japanese and what appear to be local remains, the team did not recover any U.S. remains or evidence on this mission. JPAC did receive remains previously turned in to the local police station that could be American remains. This evidence is currently undergoing analysis in our laboratory.

Of the numerous projects being undertaken at JPAC, Tarawa represents an example of the multifaceted

approach to coordinating complex data to a particularly difficult problem. Continued analysis of historical evidence along with maps and geographic data from a range of sources will form the basis for the next phase of the investigation so that all available and pertinent data can be corroborated to make the best possible assessment for future excavation operations.

INNOVATIONS

GEOGRAPHIC INFORMATION SYSTEMS

GIS is an integrated system of computer software, hardware, data, maps and personnel, which allow one to manipulate, analyze and present information that is tied to a spatial location. One of the most promising features of a GIS is that it can be used to leverage data from multiple sources simultaneously and dynamically. This enables one to efficiently obtain multiple levels of detail quickly and efficiently. Over the past several years, JPAC has been developing a Geographic Information Systems (GIS) capability framework to enhance analytical and research efforts, field planning activities and to support the identification process.

Implementation of our geospatial analysis tool has been progressing at a steady pace and the system is becoming more of an integral part of JPAC's data management, intelligence, and operation planning tool suite. The mechanical aspects of the GIS program consist of the Web GIS, the Mobile GIS, and desktop applications.

Web GIS

Web GIS is the primary portal for access to the myriad of data maintained at JPAC. Web GIS allows the geographical display and query of all JPAC data related to the Site Incidents, Casualty Individuals, Field Activities, Operational Losses and POW Camps, set over various maps and satellite imagery through the JPAC Intranet browser. Data can be extracted in map or spreadsheet format for integration into reports, briefings, etc. Integrated hyperlinks to electronic case data enable instant access to internal electronic working documents both from the geographic interface as well as a Google Earth interface. In addition, numerous specialized projects included operational plans, site status, site prioritization, automated family update maps, and other data are accessible through the GIS dashboard.

Dr. Derek Benedix, Recovery Leader, adjusts his equipment to determine the excavation area in Khammouan province, Lao People's Democratic Republic, June 26, 2010. (JPAC Photo by U.S. Marine Sgt. Neill A. Sevelius).

Mobile GIS

Mobile GIS allows the field investigator to checkout caches of data for a specific geographic area from the Web GIS to a field Toughbook computer. The mobile GIS allows similar query and projections of the data as the Web GIS with the enhancement of being able to fully collect and edit data based on field observations. The mobile GIS includes options for an integrated GPS, laser rangefinder, and camera so that all data can be collected with consistent geographic accuracy in a mapping interface. Upon returning to the field the mobile GIS investigator can check the data back into the Web and the data can be rapidly integrated to the Web GIS for review and use by all JPAC researchers and planners.

Desktop Applications

Special research and mapping projects, integration of historic imagery, remote sensing research, and creation of map projects for command and public use are being done on GIS desktop workstations. Recent collaborations with the National Geospatial Intelligence Agency (NGA) for acquisition of multispectral and thermal data to search for aircraft wreckage or the creation of excavation maps for the RTs in Tarawa are just two examples of how data are being collected and used with the GIS and other software to support the JPAC mission.

RECORDS ARCHIVES

In FY10, the J2 Records Archive was given the capability of ordering Individual Deceased Personnel Files (IDPFs) directly from the Washington National Records Center (WNRC) in Suitland, Maryland. This has enabled a more streamlined process for obtaining records to be used in the analytical process. Our records staff made two trips to the National Personnel Records Center (NPRC) in St. Louis, Missouri to obtain Official Medical Personnel Files (OMPFs) and is in the process of copying and returning to the NPRC OMPFs borrowed in previous years.

HONOLULU, Hawaii (Sept. 17, 2010) - Members of the Joint POW/MIA Accounting Command present a wreath during the POW/MIA Recognition Day ceremony held at the National Memorial Cemetery of the Pacific. The ceremony, hosted by the Joint POW/MIA Accounting Command, honored former American Prisoners of War who suffered the hardships of enemy captivity and those still Missing in Action (JPAC photo by Mass Communications Specialist 2nd Class Chris A. Perkins).

JPAC continues to obtain a significant number of IDPFs and other files which are reproduced and made available for research at JPAC. This includes large numbers of files supporting the efforts to identify individuals buried as Unknowns in the Punchbowl Cemetery, Tarawa, and other areas throughout the world. We consolidated South East Asia files and updated the inventory in the STAR Archive database system. With the assistance of the Geographic Information Systems (GIS) team in the Intelligence Directorate, JPAC has also conducted an inventory of our map collection. The consolidation helps us with our space issue (too many records, too little space dedicated for records); updating the database inventory gives us more intellectual control over our holdings.

PUNCHBOWL PROJECT

JPAC's ultimate objective for the Punchbowl Project is to exhume and identify Korean War Unknowns from the National Memorial Cemetery of the Pacific, Honolulu, Hawaii. JPAC historians use primary and secondary historical sources, along with GIS mapping analysis, to create lists of possible name associations for each Unknown case based on geography, burial/recovery date, individual loss dates, the battlefield situation, and unique evidence present in each file. The key aspect of the historical review has been the collection and processing of primary source material from the National Archives and Records Administration (NARA).

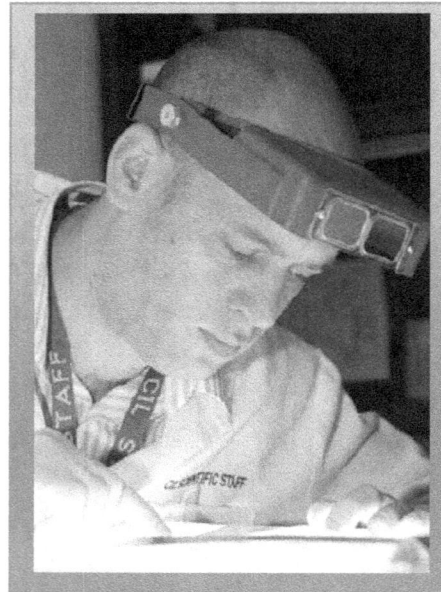

HONOLULU, Hawaii (Mar. 25, 2010) - Dr. Carl Stephan, an Anthropologist currently assigned to the Joint POW/MIA Accounting Command's Central Identification Laboratory, uses a light table to examine a chest radiograph from the Korean War era. (JPAC photo by U.S. Navy 2nd Class Petty Officer Chris A. Perkins).

To date over 80,000 pages from the Korean War Army-AG Command reports have been reviewed, photographed, and made available for command wide use on the JPAC internal file system. These documents have not only been used to create name association lists for pending exhumations, but have led to the correction of loss locations and dates for unresolved casualties which have been in error since the cases were first put together in the 1950s. The historical aspect of the Punchbowl Project is an evolving and continuous program with research trips to NARA and participation in Investigative Team missions to the Republic of Korea planned for Fiscal Year 2011. It is the overall goal of the program to generate enough leads and evidence to successfully exhume and identify two Korean War Unknowns a month until all workable cases are exhausted.

Historical analysis is being combined with laboratory analyses as well as contributions from amateur analysts to produce leads on the identities of Punchbowl Cemetery Unknowns. The leads are evaluated by laboratory management and presented to the Deputy to the Commander for CIL Operations for approval. Several exhumation requests have been drafted this year and several more are in development at this time.

IDENTIFICATION OF SKELETAL REMAINS USING CHEST RADIOGRAPHS

For the past couple of years, JPAC's Central Identification Laboratory (CIL) has been working on developing new ways to identify servicemen from the Korean War and World War II. One method at the forefront of this endeavor involves the comparison of chest radiographs with remains to determine a match. This method has the potential to enable the identification of individuals that cannot be identified using other methods (e.g., mitochondrial DNA and dental records) and is especially important in the military context because most soldiers were subject to chest radiography upon recruitment/discharge. All of the above mentioned items apply to U.S.-unknowns buried in the National Memorial Cemetery of the Pacific and thus the methods possess special significance for the identification of these human remains. Standardized and validated methods to identify skeletal remains via comparisons to antemortem chest radiographs are being derived. This project deals with both morphoscopic (qualitative visual) and morphometric (quantitative computer-based) methods partly due to the low resolution and grainy nature of the photofluorographs representing unaccounted-for U.S. personnel from WWII and Korea.

Thus far, JPAC's morphoscopic methods have been tested and validated, and our results are being published in the Journal of Forensic Sciences in May, 2011. A Standard Operating Procedure (SOP) has been written and published internally for JPAC-CIL casework. We are currently establishing competency tests for using the chest radiograph SOP. Additionally, a morphometric version of the above method using 3D clavicle scans is being produced in collaboration with Pacific North West National Laboratories and the software for this method was delivered to the JPAC-CIL at the end of November, 2010. Studies on the difference in shape acquisition between 3D bone scans and conventional 2D x-ray images (on the same bones) is underway.

We are also making advances in the collection and digitization of radiographs for this project. Currently, about 14,200 antemortem chest radiographs of unaccounted-for individuals (representing about 7,200 individuals) requested from the NARA have been electronically catalogued, re-housed in proper archival storage media, and imaged in digital format. The digital databases/collections arising from this process are currently being vetted. These will soon be rolled over into JPAC's central database system. Deteriorated (channeled) radiographs are currently being sent to Chicago Albumen works to be restored and imaged in digital format. Currently, about one-third of the 1,000 radiographs requiring this process have been completed.

THE VALUE OF CRANIOFACIAL SUPERIMPOSITION FOR THE IDENTIFICATION OF SKELETAL REMAINS

We are working to determine how craniofacial superimposition can potentially help identify skeletons when skulls and antemortem facial photographs exist and can be used when other identification methods cannot be (e.g., mitochondrial DNA, dental records, radiographs). Craniofacial superimposition appears to hold the most benefit for exclusion (determining people to whom the remains do not belong). Standardized and validated morphoscopic (qualitative visual) methods to match skulls to 2D facial photographs are being derived. Thus far, we have proposed a morphoscopic method for craniofacial superimposition and an Institution Review Board (IRB) application is currently underway to the Tripler Army Medical Center's Department of Clinical Investigation to perform a CAT scan on living volunteers to acquire skull data of known subjects as required for validation tests.

SKELETAL TRAUMA PATTERNS IN A VIETNAM ERA AIRCRAFT LOSS

Anthropologists who have examined more than one case resulting from an aircraft loss anecdotally note the presence of similar trauma. Yet, in working in the blind and writing anthropology reports on these cases, there is a lack of supporting data to interpret any observed trauma. Specifically, most available literature is based on autopsy reports, which describe trauma in broad strokes that provides little data of value to physical anthropologists. This project attempts to fill this gap by describing the patterns of skeletal trauma exhibited in the Army of the Republic of Vietnam (ARVN) collection. This collection provides a unique dataset that can be used to describe trauma resulting from the loss of individuals in a C-123 aircraft crash in 1965. The project is proceeding in two parts with the first examining lower extremity trauma (femur, tibia, and fibula) and the second examining upper extremity trauma (humerus, radius, and ulna).

Once the collection has been fully examined, it is hoped that any patterns that emerge can serve as a basis from which anthropologists can compare and contrast trauma occurring in different types of aircraft losses thus aiding their analyses and providing better results in their reports. Though at this point, it is realized there are some similarities between the patterns observed and trauma resulting from automobile crashes.

The first phase of this project can be considered complete with all trauma having been observed and described from the lower extremities. Additionally, photographs of all key elements and specific trauma patterns have been completed (though the possibility for reshoots remains). Presently, the data are being collated for presentation in a poster at the American Academy of Forensic Science (AAFS) and eventually will be written up as a subsequent publication. The second phase of the project will begin after the completion of the first phase sometime in early 2011.

Sex Determination using Patella Measurements

Anthropologists at the CIL often are called upon to study fragmentary remains on which standard analytic methods (based on complete elements) cannot be used. The patella, or kneecap, is a small and dense bone that is often recovered intact or nearly intact as part of larger fragmentary assemblages making it a strong candidate for study. The project as originally imagined (in late 2007) sought to test the accuracy and reliability of all available methods using patella measurements (height, width, thickness) to determine sex. Now it focuses on the introduction of a new patella sex determination method for use with American remains and a validation of that method using a separate dataset.

Although usually thought to be of little diagnostic potential and simply overlooked beyond possible pathological variation, a limited number of projects have indicated size differences between male and female patellae. Unfortunately, these methods are based on European, African, and Iranian samples, which may make their use in other populations questionable. American remains have been examined in only two projects. One of these studies used CT data and cannot easily be applied in a laboratory setting, and the second is presented in the unpublished Master's thesis of Gayle O'Connor, which is not widely known or used in the field. The data from the O'Connor thesis is available (300 White and Black males and females from the Terry Collection) and was originally the basis for this study. Later it was decided that additional samples were required to provide a more objective assessment of all currently available methods. This required a research trip to the Hamann-Todd collection at the Cleveland Museum of Natural History where another 180 White and Black male and female patellae were examined.

Using this data it will be possible to address the validity, accuracy, and applicability of all previous method using an independent sample. The method developed using various combinations of the three standard patellar measurements obtains accuracy percentages of 80% which drop to the mid 70% upon validation using the O'Connor Data.

Essentially JPAC's Patella Measurement Project is complete and the data has been analyzed. Data from this study will be collated and arranged for a second poster at the AAFS and a subsequent publication. The potential for a subsequent project examining the efficacy of the other methods available also remains promising as initial results indicate some differences.

Stature Determination using Patella Measurements

This project is an offshoot of the patella sex project and looks at the feasibility of using patella measurements to estimate stature. Simply stated nearly every bone in the body can be used to estimate stature, but the smaller the bone, the less precise the estimate obtained and the wider the resulting upper and lower boundaries of stature will be. Acknowledging this error, there is still potential for a stature estimation method to be used when other methods are inapplicable.

As indicated above, the patella sex project has been ongoing since late 2007, but this project developed in mid-2009. While reviewing the patella data from O'Connor it was noticed that a number of cases were repeated in the Forensic Data Bank (FDB). After combining the datasets and adding additional cases from the Byrd and Adams commingling study, a sufficient number of cases were present to permit the creation of equations to determine stature from patella measurements.

The equations developed at this point are "preliminary" equations but they have been used on a series of random test cases in the JPAC laboratory. The results of this limited testing show accurate point estimates and expected wide ranges, but in one instance the estimates developed would have segregated a taller from shorter individual in a commingled assemblage. If these were the only bones available for analysis, this data may have been sufficient when combined with mtDNA evidence to permit identifications to go forward.

Additional data obtained during a trip to the Hamann-Todd collection at the Cleveland Museum of Natural History will be used to test and refine the method. The results obtained to date can be considered as essentially equivalent to other stature estimation methods in the literature that use small bones and fragmentary remains. This suggests there may be some utility in the method. JPAC will continue our work in this area and explore the potential of this approach.

SEX DETERMINATION USING SUPRAMEATAL SPINE/DEPRESSION VARIATION

This project examines whether variation in expression of the suprameatal depression/spine (SMD-S) can be used to differentiate males from females. The SMD-S refers to a structure on the lateral surface of the temporal bone immediately behind the external auditory meatus (a tube running from the outer ear to the middle ear). The potential of this project is to provide a new tool that can be used to ascertain sex from fragmentary cranial remains.

When cranial remains are preserved, they often include the temporal bone with external auditory meatus and SMD-S as the petrous portion (hard portion of the temporal bone that forms a protective case for the inner ear) is a good candidate for mtDNA sampling. Although many study cases are available on the JPAC-CIL lab floor, a large known population was unavailable. This changed in mid-2009 when two anthropologists from the JPAC-CIL collected data from the Chiba (modern Japanese) collection. This dataset included lateral views of crania from which it was possible to code SMD-S expression. Additional data on the SMD-S was obtained during the recent data Hamann-Todd research trip.

This dataset has not been examined fully but preliminary results from the data available do suggest the concept is promising. Further work is needed to determine whether the method can be used in sex determination.

K208

The group of remains known as "K208" consists of 208 boxes of remains turned over by the DPRK in the early 1990s. These boxes were each purported to contain a single U.S. serviceman. Upon receipt of the remains it was discovered that there were often multiple individuals in each box and that the remains were extensively commingled. Approximately 350 mtDNA sequences have been found to be present in these 208 boxes of remains.

The purpose of the K208 project is to resolve the commingling present in this assemblage. The sorting process is conducted at the "village" level (the purported geographical component of the remains). They are cut for mtDNA testing and the results are then used to determine which bones share the same sequence. Anthropological analysis is conducted to compare the morphology, developmental state, and taphonomic state of the remains. Pair matches and articulations, as well as use of osteometric sorting techniques are then applied. At this time, over 42 accessions from three villages representing 68 different mtDNA sequences have been completed.

HONOLULU, Hawaii (Sept. 17, 2010) - Kahu Curtis Kekuna offers blessings to former Prisoners of War and those still missing in action during the POW/MIA Recognition Day ceremony held at the National Memorial Cemetery of the Pacific. The ceremony, hosted by the Joint POW/MIA Accounting Command, honored former American Prisoners of War who suffered the hardships of enemy captivity and those still Missing in Action (JPAC photo by Mass Communications Specialist 2nd Class Chris A. Perkins)

Current and future research in this project includes an expansion of the osteometric sorting technique to allow for the evaluation of vertebral elements, a review of methods used for determining the number of individuals present in a commingled assemblage, and the construction of a large, comprehensive database concerning these remains. The database will contain a catalog of every bone in the assemblage, to include its physical description, osteometric measurements, mtDNA sequence data, and a subsection that will allow the plotting of the geospatial and temporal relationships between these accessions.

PUBLICATIONS

The JPAC staff is composed of many of the best and brightest professionals in the fields of Forensics, History and Geographic Information Systems (GIS). This year, in addition to maintaining a significant mission workload, our staff published nine papers and presented (or submitted abstracts for) 22 presentations and/or posters at conferences on topics ranging from the applications of GIS in the accounting mission to skeletal identification by radiographic comparison.

Continued interaction with other professionals in their respective fields ensures that our staff stays current with advances being made in the private sector and ensures that any gains JPAC makes in the sciences can be visible to the industry. JPAC will continue to make it a priority for our professionals to stay up-to-date with their colleagues in the private sector so that we can ensure the most advanced and contemporary methods and innovations can be applied to solving cases involving America's fallen.

LOST DOG TAG PROJECT

Dr. Robert Mann, the Director of JPAC's Forensic Science Academy and former Laboratory Deputy Director, began the dog tag project more than 10 years ago as a humanitarian effort to reunite "lost" dog tags with their owners, primarily soldiers who served during the Vietnam War.

The process of returning a dog tag to its owner or their family begins with our notifying the National Personnel Records Center (NPRC) of a new dog tag name. The NPRC then conducts research on 40 and 50 year old records to locate information about the individual named on the dog tag. If contact information can be acquired, the NPRC writes a letter informing the individual or their next of kin that their dog tag(s) are at the JPAC-CIL in Hawaii. Individuals are instructed to directly contact JPAC to make arrangements to have it returned.

Before JPAC returns any dog tag, we verify that the dog tag is truly being matched with the right individual or family. To accomplish this, we corroborate information embossed on the tag such as, name, service number or social security number, dates of service, religion and blood type to confirm a match exists. In addition to verifying this basic info, we also try to learn about the circumstances that may have surrounded the loss of the dog tag. We may also ask questions related to when the individual served, where they were stationed, if they were wounded, and where they visited in the country, where they wore their dog tag (neck or boot) and if they recall the circumstances under which the tag was lost. JPAC includes this history in a letter accompanying the dog tag when we mail it back to its owner.

To date the CIL has thus far returned 161 of approximately 2,000 dog tags. Some are happy to be reunited with their lost tags. Other dog tags are returned to family members who are reminded of the passing of the beloved owner of the dog tag. JPAC appreciates making connections with those that served and returned from Vietnam and is proud to tell their stories through this special project.

FORENSIC SCIENCE ACADEMY

The Forensic Science Academy (FSA), established in August 2008, is an advanced forensic anthropology program facilitated by JPAC. The curriculum consists of five courses taught in the fall or spring: Archaeological Techniques, Forensic Anthropology, Quality Assurance, Evidence Handling and Laboratory Accreditation. While the courses focus on a variety of topics in anthropology related to forensic science, this program provides participants with the necessary skills and knowledge to find, recover, and identify human remains and material evidence, especially as they relate to Americans missing as a result of past wars and conflicts. All courses are taught under the auspices of the Department of Defense. The Fellows are selected from a highly competitive pool of applicants and receive two months of intensive training in forensic anthropology and archaeology at the JPAC CIL in Hawaii, followed by a five-week mission to the LPDR or Vietnam with search and recovery teams as they excavate U.S. crash sites or graves. Their program ends with a one-week long stay in Thailand studying human skeletal and dental variation at Khon Kaen Medical School. Through this experience, the students can earn credits through their respective schools. Additionally, the FSA has rapidly become the primary recruiting and training opportunity for attracting new scientists to the JPAC CIL. We hope to attract more FSA graduates to positions on the scientific staff, as well as increase the knowledge, skills and abilities of our JPAC team.

A Forensic Science Academy Fellow augmented with the Joint POW/MIA Accounting Command fills buckets with dirt during an excavation in the Savannakhet Province, Lao People Democratic Republic November 11. (JPAC photo by U.S. Marine Corps Sgt. Rebekah M. Ide).

The first class of four Fellows met from August - December 2008. The students were selected from the California State University at Chico, the

University of Florida and Michigan State University. While they enjoyed all aspects of their training at the JPAC Central Identification Laboratory (CIL), the highlight of their experience was their mission to the Lao People's Democratic Republic (LPDR) where, under the mentorship of a JPAC Recovery Leader, the Fellows gained valuable hands-on experience by participating in an actual excavation.

The Forensic Science Academy Class of 2009 consisted of six advanced masters and doctoral students from Texas State, The Ohio State University, State University of New York (SUNY) Buffalo, SUNY Binghamton, University of Florida, and Simon Fraser University.

In August of 2009, JPAC hired two anthropologists from the first graduating class and one graduate from the second class of our Forensic Science Academy into permanent positions on the scientific staff. The FSA Academy program is in its 3rd year. The current fellows in the program for 2010 are:

Julia Fan, MA, MSc - University of Massachusetts
Tim Gocha, MSc - Ohio State University
Suzanne Johnson, MA - University of Tennessee
Lara McCormick, MA - Ohio State University
Brian Schottenkirk, MA - University College, London
Traci Van Deest, MA - University of Florida

This year, the six Fellows will be presenting on a variety of forensic anthropology topics at Khon Kaen University (KKU) School of Medicine in Thailand. These fellows will also be examining the large skeleton collection at KKU during the "Workshop in Forensic Anthropology." Along with the fellows, Dr. Robert Mann, FSA Director and Dr. John Byrd, Laboratory Director will be giving a two-day presentation in Osteometrics and Advances in Forensic Anthropology for KKU students, faculty and staff.

NEGOTIATIONS

JPAC has continued talks with foreign governments in order to enable and enhance our operations abroad. In fiscal year 2010, JPAC leaders held formal negotiation and coordination meetings with officials from the Lao People's Democratic Republic (LPDR), the Kingdom of Cambodia (KOC), the Socialist Republic of Vietnam (SRV), the People's Republic of China (PRC), the Republic of Korea (ROK), and Papua New Guinea (PNG). We also traveled to India to meet informally with U.S. government officials in that country with the goal of resuming operations there.

In August, consistent with bilateral agreements between JPAC and the Ministry of Defense Agency for Killed in Action Recovery and Identification (MAKRI), we participated in a Joint Forensic Review in which remains were evaluated to determine their racial affiliation.

In conjunction with our operations in the Republic of Kiribati (Tarawa), we finalized and signed a Memorandum for the Record to enhance our operations in that nation.

Following our visit to Papua New Guinea (PNG) last fall, JPAC delivered cameras, global positioning system units, and computers to our counterparts in the PNG Museum of Natural History to enhance PNG's capacity to support JPAC operations. The transfer of such equipment and training to the PNG National Museums authorized under Section 1207, Chapter 20, Sub-section 408 of Title 10 United States Code "Authority to Equip and Train Foreign Personnel to

TSgt. Julie Lujan, Team Medic for Recovery Team 2, teaches children how to brush their teeth in the Khammouan province, Lao People's Democratic Republic, July 11, 2010. (JPAC Photo by U.S. Marine Sgt. Neill A. Sevelius).

Assist in Accounting for Missing United States Government Personnel." By participating in such "equip and train" activities, we build a stronger partnership and bilateral relationship between the United States and Papua New Guinea which will in turn benefit the mission to recover the fallen in PNG. Command visits to the LPDR, SRV, KOC, and the ROK rounded out our foreign government interactions.

FACILITIES

We made significant strides toward our $99M Military Construction (MILCON) project during FY10. Through excellent cooperation and teamwork among JPAC directorates, the design team, and NAVFAC Pacific to complete the Function Analysis and Conceptual Design (FACD) in Nov 2009, this fiscal year the 35% designs, 60% designs, and final 100% designs were successfully accomplished. Construction proposals are currently being solicited for this project and will be awarded when Congress has approved the FY2011 MILCON budget. Ground breaking is anticipated in April 2011 and the project will take 2 years to construct. The anticipated move-in date is expected to take place in 2014. This new building will consolidate JPAC operations and provide almost 140,000 total square feet (sq. ft) of space for our organization. The new space will boast 53,000 sq. ft of dedicated laboratory area; more than double the current space at both our Hickam and Pearl Harbor sites combined.

Long-term money saving solutions has also been a priority during FY10. Designs for installation of roof mounted, 65KW photovoltaic systems were completed for our offices at both sites. The sun-to-electricity systems are expected to save JPAC $21,000–$25,000 in annual utility costs for each building. Installation of the system for Hickam is occurring, and an installation date will be set for Pearl Harbor when all necessary approvals have been gained. In addition, a cool roof application is currently being installed at our headquarters at Hickam AFB.

We expect additional energy savings from the reduction of the building's cooling losses through the roof.

Quality of life improvements for our staff remains a priority this year and we have achieved many positive changes that will have lasting impacts to our personnel. Space currently occupied by our teams and some communications staff has undergone numerous internal repairs over the year and we are finishing up exterior repairs and painting. Additionally, we relocated our human resources and travel support staff to a location closer to our headquarters in order to better accommodate the main population of our organization. We recognized the need for our photographers to have more table space and moved them to a larger office at Pearl Harbor where they have more room for large photo layout work.

Finally, we renovated our main conference room to repair walls, improve cooling and air circulation, improve lighting, install updated communication and data systems, and replace worn flooring. This room doubles as JPAC operations center and supports hundreds of visitors including families, VIPs, and foreign officials.

A graphic rendering of JPAC's future headquarters building, planned for completion in 2014. JPAC plans to break ground at the planned building site at Joint Base Pearl Harbor-Hickam, HI in 2011.

MEDIA AND INTERNAL INFORMATION OPERATIONS

JPAC has enjoyed a high level of National & Global Media Coverage during FY10. The Korean Broadcast System (KBS) filmed a recovery operation and other segments in the Central Identification Laboratory as part of their coverage of the 60th anniversary of the Korean War. There was also significant media coverage of JPAC's Tarawa mission including three stories by CNN, two documentary pieces by Rogin Entertainment, a single documentary on JPAC in Tarawa by Steven C. Barber, and other JPAC Tarawa operations coverage by the Air Force Network (AFN) & Defense Media Activity (DMA).

National and International coverage was very positive this year. In February, a JPAC RT closed an open

JPAC Teams Forty-one years after a fatal mission, an Airman is returned to his family. Read more (via Airman Magazine) at http://bit.ly/aBhEse

Returning Home
bit.ly
In 1949, then 1st Lt. William Mason went on a blind date with a girl named Irene. He graduated from West Point just two years earlier and was among the first to join the new Air Force. There he focused on becoming the best pilot possible eventually earning the rank of colonel. Four months after that

September 30 at 8:34pm · Comment · Like · Share · Promote · Flag

Jan Zdiarsky likes this.

Paula Davis Johnson What an amazing gift you are giving the families of these American heroes!! Thank you JPAC for the wonderful work you are doing. All Americans need to be told about your work. I never knew you existed until the son of a friend joined your group. I am in awe of the work you do.
October 1 at 12:35am · Like · Flag

Susan Clotfelter Jimison I agree Paula. Americans need to know the about the talent and dedication these people at JPAC do. That was a great story about Col. Mason and his crew. RIP Col. Mason and your crew.
October 1 at 3:01am · Like · Flag

Tammy Brickley These people are wonderful. They are looking for my 2nd cousin now.
October 1 at 4:06am · Like · Flag

Write a comment...

In FY10, JPAC launched a Facebook page and currently has 300 followers. This is a screen-capture of a recent JPAC Facebook page post and associated feedback.

excavation site initiated by a civilian in search of the remains of Sean Flynn, son of Hollywood legend Errol Flynn, and other Vietnam-era journalists who went missing in April 1970. JPAC received national and international attention for the Cambodia recovery mission; the remains were subsequently determined by JPAC not to have been those of Flynn. Additionally, we received significant positive coverage in China and internationally for our participation in a media roundtable in coordination with U.S. Embassy Beijing in April. More recently, Airman Magazine, the flagship publication of the U.S. Air Force, featured JPAC in their September/October issue with a four-page spread about the repatriation of Col William Mason after 41 years of being missing when his C-130A Hercules went down in Laos.

Local media coverage was also positive this fiscal year. JPAC had stories run multiple times on Hawaii Public Radio and the Honolulu Advertiser, featuring stories about recovery and investigation operations, the dog tag project, Arrival Ceremonies, and identifications using mitochondrial DNA (mtDNA). Hawaii News Now also streamed live coverage of a JPAC Arrival Ceremony. This September, presentations at the POW/MIA Recognition Day ceremony by then Hawaii State Governor Linda Lingle and one of the founders of the National League of

POW/MIA Families, Mrs. Carole Hickerson, resulted in multiple local news agencies requesting subsequent interviews.

PUBLIC OUTREACH

This fiscal year, JPAC hosted more than 100 command and Central Identification Laboratory tours. Of that, more than 40 were U.S. VIP tours (General Officers, Senior Ranking Government Officials, Senate Staffers, and U.S. Ambassadors), about 15 were senior foreign visitors (Foreign Ambassadors, Senior Foreign Military), and about 60 general public tours. In addition, we attended several public outreach events, targeting multiple audiences

September 2010: Secretary of State, Hillary Rodham-Clinton attended at a repatriation ceremony and looks on as an American flag is draped over a casket containing remains believed to be those of a U.S. service member recovered in Vietnam.

throughout the United States and abroad. JPAC public affairs staff members reached more than 750,000 by presenting artifact and information booths or speaking at more than 10 nationwide events.

This year, we also hosted numerous private tours for family members at our headquarters and provided operational briefings and one-on-one family meetings at nine family update events in Jackson, Mississippi, Orlando, Florida, Los Angeles, California, Honolulu, Hawaii, San Antonio, Texas, Raleigh, North Carolina, Seattle, Washington, Syracuse, New York, and Omaha, Nebraska. These sessions gave us the opportunity not only to meet new family members but allowed us to provide case updates and answer specific questions about our mission.

Interaction with Congress was also significant this year. JPAC hosted visits from Congressman David Wu (OR) in January and Congressman Rick Larsen (WA) in June. We were pleased to both provide the command briefing and laboratory tour as well as discuss their specific questions about our mission and ongoing projects. Two staff members from the House

Armed Services Committee (HASC) visited excavation sites in both Vietnam and Korea in June then spent time at our headquarters in Hawaii with JPAC staff member to discuss ongoing projects, initiatives, and perceived forthcoming challenges.

Aside from meeting personally with our stakeholders, our External Relations staff handled 587 written inquiries from family members, Congress, the Service Casualty Offices, and the public. Of these, 88 were Congressional inquiries and at least 225 were from family members. This is a sharp increase from the volume of inquiries handled last fiscal year. In addition to direct telephone and email contact, the world now has access to JPAC via social media. In FY10, JPAC embraced the global social networking trend and extended our virtual network using sites such as Facebook, Twitter, Flickr, YouTube, & Delicious. JPAC also hosted "Tweet-ups" (a real world social gathering for people who know each other through the online Twitter service), and gave users an opportunity to meet in person, network, and have fun while allowing JPAC to promote the mission in a controlled setting. We currently have more than 300 followers on Facebook and encourage everyone to exchange commentary with JPAC. These social media initiatives will undoubtedly influence our opportunities for public engagement in the coming years and we will prepare to evolve with the technological advances that give the global community direct access to our organization.

LOOKING AHEAD TO THE FUTURE

The National Defense Authorization Act of 2010 contained language directing the Department of Defense to increase the number of annual identifications to 200 by the year 2015. This represents an increase of more than double the current rate of identifications.

We have begun internal evaluations to better understand the precise factors that influence our identification productivity. We have also started engaging in discussions with our counterparts across the POW/MIA community on courses of action that could help us reach this goal. It is becoming clear that to achieve this target output, a significant increase in inputs is immediately required. While the inputs needed are mostly in the form of yields from investigation and recovery missions, additional skilled personnel to interpret and process the inputs are imperative if we hope to realize this objective. Further complexities arise from the fact that JPAC is one part of a larger accounting community whose elements are subject to their own constraints and mandates.

Despite the numerous complexities associated with the task, JPAC is committed to collaboration with our counterparts to discuss approaches to attaining the goal set forth by Congress and the American people.

Until They Are Home!